Bears Live Here

# Bears Live Here

## By IRMENGARDE EBERLE

Doubleday & Company, Inc.   Garden City, New York

Irmengarde Eberle is a member of the Authors League of America.

To Kathleen and Patricia Horan
and Maude and Jane Leslie

Wild black bears are friendly with each other. But they do not like people.

Once there were thousands of them over most of America. But from the time settlers first came over from Europe, men hunted them. And bears learned that people were their enemies.

Today, most of the broad lands where once bears roamed are covered with cities, farms, mines and factories. The remaining ones live in rugged mountain and forest areas. To these places men seldom come, or not at all. Here the bears survived.

High on a mountainside covered thickly with firs, oaks and many other trees, live two such black bears.

Their den is a shallow cave in a rough wall of rock. Last autumn they pushed dry leaves into it, and made themselves a bed. Bushes and small trees stand nearby and partly hide the opening. They protect the cave a little from wind, rain and snow. Here the two bears lived quietly together for some months in the winter. Most of the time they slept, and they sucked their paws as bears do while in their winter's sleep.

They were big. He weighed nearly four hundred pounds, and she a little less. They were lean, because during the long periods of sleep they of course ate nothing at all. But their thick, warm hair made them look plump.

When February came, the female awoke and grew restless. She grunted and growled a little, and pushed at the great male with her snout. He growled back. But he was aware that it was time for him to go.

Arising slowly from his comfortable bed of leaves, he went outside. The slope on which he found himself was thinly covered with old snow partly melted, partly frozen.

The bare, gray trees around him creaked and groaned as the wind rubbed the branches together. The bear shook himself and went lumbering off. He was looking for another sheltered place where he could make his home for a while. And soon he found one in a thicket of young trees covered with a tangle of dry vines.

Back in the den in the mountain wall, two small cubs were born to the mother bear. There was a good reason why she had wanted the father to leave. For male bears are often rough and careless with their young.

The young ones were tiny—only about seven inches long. They made a faint whimpering sound. The mother moved about carefully to keep from crushing them. One of her big paws would have covered a young one completely. The cubs' eyes were closed, and they were scantily covered with short, silky, grayish hair. The mother licked them, then fell asleep again. Her winter's sleep was not yet over.

The small cubs snuggled into her warm fur. They too slept. In fact they slept most of the time in the next few weeks, awakening just long enough, every now and then, to find their mother's nipples and drink her milk.

They grew rapidly. In three weeks' time they had tripled in size. Though their eyes were still closed, they crawled around a little more inside the cave. Sometimes their mother awoke when they stirred, and watched them awhile. Then all slept again.

One day in March, the mother bear awoke fully. The long periods of sleeping were over for her. She was hungry. She fed her cubs first. Then, covering them with leaves so that no other creature should find them, she went to look for food and water for herself. She walked through the mountain forest, and came out from among the tall bare trees. As she lumbered across an open place, the sun shone warmly on her back and she felt the stirring of spring clearly. Her paws padded onward more quickly.

At last she came to a brook. Most of the ice had melted, and she waded in. She waited quietly until a fish swam close to her. Very swiftly, she snapped her strong jaws shut over it, and had her breakfast.

She caught another, then hurried back to her cubs to make sure they were safe.

For herself she had no fear. She and all her kind were the biggest animals in the forest. Her great bulk and strength, her sharp claws and teeth, were excellent weapons. But her cubs were so very small and weak, for them she had fear. Foxes were the worst enemies of very young bears. These sometimes stole the little cubs from the dens and ate them, while the mothers were away.

The mother bear had another fear—an almost forgotten one. It was the fear of people. She had seen only a few men in all her life, and that was long ago. But the fear lurked in her, ready to be aroused by certain smells and sounds.

She rose up on her hind feet before her den. She looked about her and listened, and she sniffed the air. Then she went inside to her young ones.

She went out for food often now, and all was quiet and peaceful in the forest. Her cubs stayed hidden in the cave. No fox came that way.

Once when the mother returned after a short trip, she found that one of her cubs had scrambled out to the edge of the den. There he sat among the dry leaves, holding his small head up eagerly. She grunted, and pushed him gently back with her snout. He was too young and helpless to be allowed outside.

The two young bear cubs grew rapidly. When they were almost five weeks old their eyes opened. Now they could see. They grew livelier, and full of curiosity. The cubs were as big as cats by this time, and in another couple of weeks they were as big as raccoons.

One day, when they were a little over two months old, the mother led them out of the cave. This was a great time for the small cubs, and also for the mother. She watched them every second.

Sometimes one cub was slower than the other. She stayed with the boldest for a while, then hurried back and encouraged the other one to walk a little faster.

The young ones' legs were very shaky. They tumbled often, and sometimes they just sat still. But they went on after a while. In this way they learned to make their way over the rocky ground.

The bear mother grew fatter because of the good food to be had at this season. She ate fish and young land animals of many kinds. She had been shedding her thick winter hair, and had grown a glossier, black coat. The young ones lost their baby fuzz, and grew darker hair more like their mother's.

Every day when the mother took the cubs out they walked a little better. They were developing strong muscles.

They began to stand on their hind legs, and walk that way a little—just as their mother sometimes did. And they were playful.

At first the mother kept them near the cave. But soon she took them on longer walks. She showed them new places on the mountainside. They learned where the brook was, and the grassy patches. They came to know the paths made by several bears walking there year after year. They saw deer standing in the grass, or walking along a deer trail among the trees. They saw rabbits, raccoons and porcupines. And they learned to know porcupines and stay away from them because of the danger of their quills.

They met other bears. There were several mothers with young ones around here, and they were always very friendly. Sometimes they played with the other young cubs.

The cubs watched their mother hunt for food, and began to eat some of the things she ate. They learned especially to hunt for anthills. When they and their mother found one, the mother dug it up. Then she and her young ones sucked up the ants and ate them. Ants were one of their favorite foods.

The cubs watched their mother turn stones over and look for insects underneath. These too were eaten. As the spring advanced, grass and weeds sprang up, and bushes and trees put out new leaves. Now the bear mother also had the green leaves of plants to eat. The cubs nibbled too.

Often the mother stopped and sniffed the air, and listened. Her ears and nose were better than her eyes. She could smell odors, or hear sounds, from very far off, especially if the wind blew the scent or sound toward her. She must always be alert.

They did not go back to the den in the evenings, but slept in hidden places in the brush or under the sweeping branches of young pines.

The cool of the mountain nights did not bother them, nor the dew. The stones and sticks and fir needles under them when they slept were not uncomfortable. Their thick fur cushioned and warmed them.

Sometimes they wandered about in the dark too.

One day the mother left her cubs at the bottom of a tall tree, and climbed up into its branches. She had seen a squirrel leave its nest, and knew there were young ones up there. She did not try to catch the grown squirrels. They were swift, and climbed on thin branches where a bear could not follow. But the young ones—that was a different matter. The bear reached the nest quickly, and took it apart with her big paws. She picked up the little squirrels and dropped them down for her cubs to eat.

The cubs, having seen their mother climb a tree, tried it too. At first it was too much for them. They clawed into the bark and tried to pull themselves up, but they tumbled down. One day, however, the little female cub got all the way to the first crotch of a tree. There she sat and looked about fearfully. She found it hard to get back down to the ground a little later.

The other one—the male cub—climbed too. Both went higher each day. Finally one of them reached the very topmost branch of a small tree. And he held on firmly as the branch rocked and swung under his weight.

But it was the mother who climbed for food. It was she who brought down young birds and squirrels. The cubs did not know how to do that yet.

Always when they were out walking, the mother kept her cubs close to her. When one of them went too far from her, she went after him and cuffed him a little to make him come back.

When she lay down to rest they nuzzled her, or tumbled over her in play. She gently pushed them over, playing too. Or she rolled them on the ground with her big paws.

Still more, the young ones romped with each other. Sometimes they stood up on their hind legs and wrestled. Sometimes they hit at each other in their play, like two small prizefighters. They nibbled each other's ears and paws. And they tumbled on the ground together.

More and more they hunted food for themselves. They dug in the ground for grubs and roots. They pounced on frogs, and took the young from the nests of field mice, rabbits and birds that nested on the ground. They ate all the insects they could find.

The mother made soft grunting sounds. Her young ones were doing what she wanted them to.

One morning one of them saw an insect crawling out of a log. He ate it, and then peeled the bark away with his claws, looking for more. Disturbed, the insects crawled this way and that. He licked them up. He scratched again, but he got a splinter in his foot, and had to nibble at that until he got it out. Then he was through with the log that had hurt him and went off to look for something else to do.

Both the cubs still needed their mother's milk. After a few hours of lively play, and of eating, they came to her. She was always ready for them, big though they were. Sometimes she sat up on her hind legs while they nursed. Other times she lay down with them.

Often the cubs would fall asleep after nursing. In the half-shade under a tree, they would lie side by side.

Their mother sat nearby, watching over them. Or she walked about close by, her ears, eyes and nose alert.

As the summer days grew long and warm there were new young animals and fresh green things to eat. Once the bear mother saw a young deer who was separated from its mother at the moment. She killed it with a blow of her great paw, and she and her cubs devoured it. But always she killed only what they needed for food.

Another time the mother took her cubs a mile or more down the mountain, looking for insects and plants she liked. In the valley they passed a daisy patch and saw their father standing among the flowers. The cubs did not know they were related to him.

The mother was no longer afraid he would hurt her young ones. They were quite big and strong, and could take care of themselves better now. Still, she paid no attention to the male bear.

Mother and cubs came to a rocky creek bed. Here the young ones romped about.

The mother sat and rested. The wind was not in the right direction, and so she did not hear or smell the man and dog who were coming toward them. Suddenly these strangers stepped into the dry creek bed quite close to the bears. The mother saw the man and instantly drew up her paws and snarled, baring her sharp teeth.

The man had no gun. Wise enough to be afraid of a bear, and especially one with cubs, he started away from there fast. The dog barked furiously. But he knew enough not to attack so large and angry an animal. He ran back a little way with the man, then stood still, barking again.

Meanwhile the bear mother had called her two young ones to her with low grunts, growls and whines. "Danger!" she seemed to say. "Danger!"

The cubs came instantly, and she bumped them with her snout, and pushed them with her paws. In this way she got them to climb up a tree where they would be safer.

Then she turned, and with an angry growl chased the man and dog. Over the rocky ground she went, through brush, and among tall trees. When she had them well on the run, and thoroughly frightened, she stopped. She watched them for a moment longer. Then she hurried back to her cubs.

She grunted them down out of the tree and, at a fast trot, led them deeper into the woods—away from where man and dog had been. She zigzagged and circled back on herself now and then, to throw the man and dog off, should they return and follow.

Mother and cubs ran briskly. At last, in a secret, hidden place in the tree-covered, rugged mountains, the big bear stopped. She and her young ones might be safe here.

They waited for a long time, the cubs staying close to their mother. The big bear sniffed and listened. When she was certain there was no sound or smell of dog or man, she let her cubs wander about and play again.

There was still much of the day left and, after a while, they set out to look for food as before.

The mother took the cubs to a small shallow lake, where they had come only a few times before. Here she went for a swim. The two cubs were surprised, for she swam far out into deeper water than usual. They sat down on the grassy, weedy bank and watched her, eager to be with her, afraid to venture out.

At last they stepped in at the edge and tried to swim as she did. It was great sport even though they were not good at it yet. Mostly they waded and bathed. And playing, they went along close to the shore.

They came to a weedy strip at the water's edge. Here they got out and shook themselves, making the water drops fly around them like a shower.

Some other wet young bear cubs were already there on the shore, and came to play with them. But then their mother took them off into the woods.

Our two cubs' mother came along soon. She had a big fish in her mouth which she had caught in a shallow place near shore. Looking about to make sure no other animal was near to steal the food, she dropped it before her cubs. They ate.

Later they all sunned themselves, and their hair grew dry again. The mother rooted about with her nose close to the ground. The cubs kept near the water—it fascinated them.

Finally their mother led them away.

Weeks passed, and more new and pleasant things happened in the cubs' lives. One day their mother got the scent of honey on the air. She followed her nose, and it led her to a hollow tree in which wild bees had made their hive. Her cubs now smelled the wonderful smell of honey too, and eagerly joined her.

The mother bear climbed up to the hole in the tree, and put her arm down into it. But she could not reach the hive. She came down and knocked on the tree trunk, and listened. At one spot it sounded less hollow. She knew the hive was there. Then, with her mighty paws and claws, she tore the outer wood away and laid the hive bare.

She ate a little, fighting off the stinging bees as best she could. Then grunting to her cubs who were hungrily watching, she let them eat. How the bees stung! But the honey was too good, and the cubs did not leave. This was the best meal they had ever had.

After that the young ones often hunted for honey themselves. But seldom were they successful. It was usually the mother who found it.

It grew hot. The bears swam or waded in the brook or lake more than ever. And the mother fished there as usual. The young ones began to learn to fish too. They gave up drinking their mother's milk, and lived entirely on other foods.

One day in July a large male bear came and joined the family. The mother did not object to him, for by this time her cubs were really wonderfully strong, and in no danger from any male bear. Besides, the cubs did not need her quite so much, and so she had some time for the male.

She welcomed him with soft grunts. Then the whole group went on through the forest together. It was mating time, and many bears in widely scattered places in the forest were getting together in pairs.

Berries grew ripe. The bears liked these very much and often went looking for them in the sunny, open patches on the lower slopes of the mountain. Blueberries were the best kind. When they found some, the bears went in among the bushes and ate their fill.

Once as they came to their favorite patch, they found several other bears already there. These looked up at the newcomers, as though glad to have their company. But then all the bears paid little attention to each other. Each was too busy eating berries.

Nuts ripened on the trees. These too the bears liked to eat. They

climbed into trees, and broke off branches that were full of nuts. The branches dropped with a rustle and a thud. Again the bears climbed young saplings, just bearing their first full crops. The little trees bent over with the big bears' weight, and finally they snapped. This was what the bears wanted. Nuts were easier to pick off broken saplings or branches from the ground.

The adult male and female bears often scratched the bark of trees. The cubs did too. Bits of bark flew left and right. Everywhere in the forest the bears left their marks of broken branches and clawed bark.

The cubs grew more and more independent. Their mother didn't try to stop them. But much of the time she still watched them. She usually took them along when she went looking for food, or for a swim. The cubs were quite big now, but it would be four years before they were fully adult.

One afternoon mother and cubs walked very far down a mountain slope —farther than they had ever gone before. They slept in the woods, and walked more miles when they were rested.

One of the cubs went so far ahead of the others that he could no longer see them or hear them. He found himself a sunny place and sat down and waited. After a while he heard the swish and crackle of branches and leaves, the pad of bear paws, and knew his family was nearby. With a mischievous look on his face, he waited another moment, then got up and ran on, just far enough ahead to keep out of their sight.

Then he smelled something wonderful on the breeze. It was honey again! But where? He followed the scent, and after a long walk far down the mountain, he came upon a man-made beehive. This was something new to him. But as long as it had honey in it he did not question how it got there.

The hive belonged to a farmer down in the valley. His farm was far away from other houses or towns. He had put his hive in his car and taken it up into the mountains because he thought there were more blooming plants and grasses here from which his bees could get honey.

The big bear cub went over to the hive and looked it over. It was made of hard, smooth boards, and he saw no way of opening it. He tipped it. The bees came out and began to swarm around him and sting him. He fought them off, but kept on scratching and slapping at the hive. He must have that honey.

By this time the mother bear and the other cub had caught up with him. The mother was growling because she smelled that a man had been here. She stood on her hind legs, looked about her, and sniffed and listened. Certainly no man was near just now. All seemed safe. She and the second cub then came to help the first one.

The mother felt all over the hive with her paws, and found the latches which held the top down. These she raked open with a swift motion. Then the honeycomb lay before them, and all three took turns clawing it out and eating.

When they had finished, there was nothing left of the farmer's honey. The bees went off excitedly, not knowing yet where they would make their next home.

Sticky with sweet honey, but pleasantly satisfied, the three bears trotted off up the mountain, and were soon far from this place where a man had once been.

A few more weeks and the leaves turned brown, red and gold, all except the fir trees which stood out in strong, dark greens.

The mother and the male bear were often alone together now. They would hunt food, or lumber along on their walks together. Often they just sat or stood near each other in the weeds and grasses and looked about them, and listened to the sounds of the autumn forest.

All the bears shed their summer hair, which had become a little rough and shaggy. They grew a thick new crop which would keep them warm enough through the cold winter months that lay ahead. They ate a great deal, and put on more and more fat. They would need this through the winter too. The male now weighed five hundred pounds, the female more than a hundred pounds less.

Ice formed on the brook. It was time to find shelters for the winter. The mother did not want her two big cubs to stay in the same den with her, but she wanted them nearby. She set out to look for a den for them. By scratching a few loose rocks away, she made the hollow under a rock ledge a little deeper. Here she and the young ones raked in leaves with their paws. Now the big cubs had a home of their own.

The mother went off to her old den. The male bear found a cave for himself. At first they only slept part of the time, and still hunted for food.

Then bitter winter weather set in. The ground was frozen so hard that it felt like rock under the bears' big, flat paws. Snow came, and wind blew it through the forest and around the mountain crags in great swirls. The adult bears settled down in their dens. The two cubs in their own snuggled against each other and kept each other warm. All slept for long periods in partial hibernation.

Next spring the mother bear would have new cubs—perhaps three or four, but most likely two. The big ones of this season would follow her part of the time when she came out of the den with her new cubs. But if they kept close to her for too long, she would cuff them and make them go away. For in the second spring they would be old enough to be independent.

Strong, big and bulky, they would be ready for the world in which they lived. The world of dangerous men lay far off in the distance somewhere. Here was a world of rocks and trees, and of small wild animals of which bears were not afraid. And most of the bears would live here peacefully for the twenty years or more of their life span.

A Texan by birth, Irmengarde Eberle came east shortly after graduating from college and became an editor and a writer of adult articles and fiction.

Miss Eberle's greatest interest, however, lies in writing books for young people—and particularly in portraying animals in warm presentations that combine accurate natural history with playful fiction. She has written over forty books for children.

Miss Eberle exercises great care and much time in selecting photographs for her books, utilizing several sources. She feels that no single photographer can catch a truly wild animal in all its stages of growth, and in a wide range of activities and situations.

She and her husband, Arnold W. Koehler, live in New York City. They also have a home far out on Long Island, and although there aren't any black bears, many kinds of wild animals do live there.

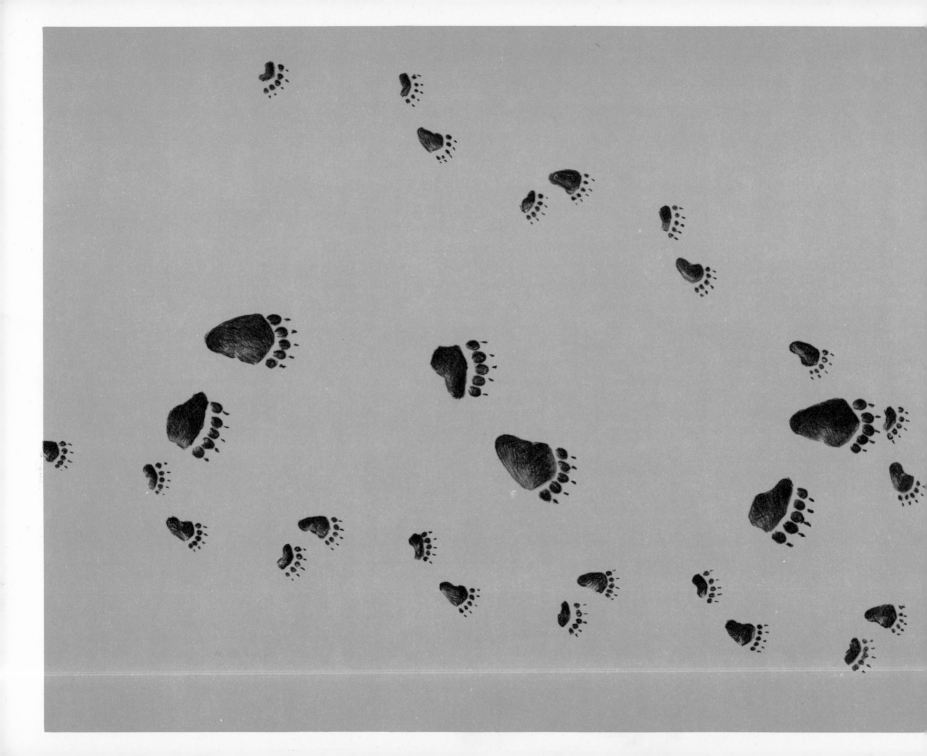